Listening Circles: Seeding Life

A Guide to Facilitating Women's Circles in Community

Anne's experiences illustrate the life-giving power of women gathering, listening and touching into the power of silence. This book, punctuated with beautiful quotes, poetry and personal memories, outlines the basics of gathering in circle, but more importantly, creates a longing for creating such sacred moments.

— WENDY HERSCHMAN, Executive Director,
The Red Shoes, A Center for Personal & Spiritual Growth

Anne Scott has refined the ability to listen deeply to her dreams and to the subtle world of women's true nature. She communicates her own trust that a natural inner compass is available to those who in their outer lives may be experiencing the extremes of alienation and abandonment.

In this beautiful little book, Anne teaches us to trust our natural inner compass, and to bear gentle witness to what emerges from the inner worlds. There is no interference, no effort in this work—we simply create a space. Here we are guided to an attitude of respect and reverence for the light that can come to women through befriending themselves. And we participate as well, in touching something luminous.

— HOLLY JAVADI, M.A., Therapist,
International Rescue Committee

Reading this guide, I found myself reflecting that this kind of welcoming, this way of being with one another, is what is needed in our lives. It shows us a profoundly important way of holding in our hearts and welcoming all whom we meet—whether in circles, with friends, with families, or in ourselves and in nature. This gracious hospitality embodies a particular kind of light. This book is both an insightful guide for holding groups, and a true guide for living during these difficult and dark times.

— KAREN JURGENS, M.S., L.P.
Retired Licensed Psychologist &
Marriage & Family Therapist

This book is a heartfelt offering born out of love, respect for all people, a deeply feminine and profound perspective, and the author's body of extensive experience working with women. I trust that many people will benefit from this offering.

—MARIANA CAPLAN, PHD, author of *Yoga & Psyche: Integrating the Paths of Yoga and Psychology for Healing, Transformation, and Joy*

Listening Circles: Seeding Life

*A Guide to Facilitating Women's Circles
in Community*

Anne Scott

with Diana Badger

NICASIO PRESS

Listening Circles: Seeding Life

Anne Scott

with Diana Badger

All inquiries should be addressed to:
Anne Scott
DreamWeather Foundation
P.O. Box 2002, Sebastopol, CA 95473

www.dreamweather.org

Cover design: Patti Buttitta

First published in the United States by
Nicasio Press
Sebastopol, California
www.nicasiopress.com
Printed in the United States of America
ISBN 979-8-9897756-1-3

Awaken wisdom within,
and let it flow out to the world
like a gardener
sowing seeds of life.

— NAN MERRILL

CONTENTS

FOREWORD

Having been involved in Anne Scott's prior book about the work of Listening Circles, I came to understand that this work is not just for women who are facing existential crises due to homelessness, and not just in California. Those in crisis include refugees in Germany (currently from Ukraine), and many countries; people in emergency situations because of the outcome of the COVID-19 situation; those facing unemployment; or people with life-threatening illnesses.

While Anne's work on this is a specific offering for homeless women in California, there are two basic aspects for me that I see about the experience of women that could be transferred to other contexts in a different way.

For one thing, every woman (and perhaps every man, although more difficult for some) can discover an inner treasure—a wisdom that does not come from comprehension or understanding, but from a connection to something larger than themselves.

Anne speaks often of the sacredness in each of us, which has nothing to do with religion, but rather with the experience of oneness, of a wholeness that is independent of any religious system. And she speaks of the fact that women can experience this independent of their outlook and situation. This treasure is often right under the surface, just waiting to be brought forward.

Does Anne do something "special" in order for that to happen, to create that situation? Yes and no. No, because she hardly has a technique or method, and uses very little structure. She is not "the doer," or "making it happen."

And yes, because she offers a secure empty space, within which there are no expectations.

May the stories from Anne's book touch you as well as assist you in discovering your own inner strength and power, your own "holy nature."

And may they encourage you, in your own world or circumstances, to offer something similar to your loved ones or community, thereby continuing to "pay it forward," by extending to anyone in need, not only people in a state of emergency. And, our planet, facing its own crisis, is equally in need as well.

— KLAUS UHL, psychotherapist,
German translator for
Finding Home: Restoring the Sacred to Life

INTRODUCTION

A woman is sitting quietly on the grass by the parking lot of a shelter for women experiencing homelessness. She's been coming to our circles for several months.

"I can't come today," she says. "I would just cry." I invite her to come anyway, and a few minutes later, I'm happy to see that she has decided to join us.

We meet for just an hour. In the first five minutes, I introduce myself, and the women go around the circle, stating their names and, sometimes, why they've come. Then we go into meditation. It's a simple heart meditation that I share, but always I ask the women to be in the silence in whatever way is most familiar to them.

After about five minutes, I end the meditation and look around the room. I love this time, when the women open their eyes and sense the connection within themselves, and to each other.

I say that this is a time when the women can share, if they'd like, about their experience of meditating. The woman who had been sitting by the parking lot begins speaking quietly.

"Something happened," she says. "I found a place inside that was like darkness but wasn't really dark. In that place there was no emotion. No thinking. It was so peaceful."

Her face is bright, almost shining.

This is not unusual in our circles. When a woman finds this deeper place within herself, it's like the first rain after a drought. It is undeniable. If nurtured over time, with the support of such a circle, this place inside grows resilience and strength, and an astonishing natural wisdom emerges.

Years ago, when I first began this work, my teacher told me that women have always worked together, working at a deeper level where real change takes place. Anything else, he told me, is a band-aid.

Over the next twenty-five years, I held listening circles for women at retreat centers and private venues across the country. Then, when I was invited to create a project for circles at a local day shelter for women experiencing homelessness, I wanted to see if this could work there as well. And it did. My book *Finding Home: Restoring the Sacred to Life—Stories of Women in Transition and Homelessness* offers a view of how deeply some of the women in these circles took up what was offered, and how their lives were touched.

～

It was in 2014 that I heard the prophetic words from Diane Longboat, an Indigenous leader and educator. Sitting on the carpeted floor with a small group of women, we'd been meeting for four days to share and listen to the Indigenous grandmothers. Although long ago now, there were two things that I vividly remember: hearing a dream, and the words Diane spoke about the future.

In particular, she described a dream that foretold of a cloud covering the planet, but conveyed that there was a way to not run from it—to instead face the darkness with compassion and love. This has stayed with me through the years, for once you hear a dream such as this, it penetrates like a light into one's consciousness, whether or not we can accept it rationally.

I also recall that Diane spoke about how the disruptions caused by our separation from the Earth —our loss of a sense of belonging—will see the rise of mental illnesses around the world.

And so, as I reflect on our circles for the women in the safe-parking shelter in the community where I live, I see how infinitely valuable they are in creating a sense of connection and belonging in a time of darkening. How this linking with self and other in shared space, focusing on the place of wholeness within, is itself both healing and transforming.

A woman named Janet, who has been coming to our circles every week since we began last year, is one of those who, through these group meetings, was able to experience a profound reconnection to her essential self.

With a measured, quiet voice, she made a declaration that resonated with everyone:

"If I could be anywhere, it would be here."

She looked around with a slight smile at our small circle of women who sit together on plastic chairs inside the tent, with gravel beneath our feet.

I decided to write this manual to provide guidelines and inspiration for creating and sustaining similar groups for women. In this book, I draw from experience working with those facing homelessness or transition. The manual is also designed for *any of us* to meet the ever-growing need to come together in community to share and receive support in connecting to our inner place of *home*.

This work, of "working without doing," is vital nourishment, and absolutely needs to be shared in a world of ever-increasing distractions. Groups are an important place where this capacity for deep presence can be practiced and held. It is a place where we can weave into life a dropped thread of love.

On a practical level, Listening Circles also serve to address the trauma that can be found in some who are facing homelessness or in transition, such as refugees, or those in mental health distress. The circles function not by way of directly addressing the trauma, but by focusing on the place within a woman that is inviolable, that is always whole, and is itself a source of healing.

During my work with women over the last two decades, I have had dreams to help me understand more clearly how to do this. In one unforgettable dream, a man who came from the north, and who understood the taxonomy of trees, explained to me that each tree emits a certain frequency, which nourishes the trees around it. He stressed that each tree is needed, and essential.

Just as we have a science for the taxonomy of trees, helping us to understand the natural world, so too is there a way to illuminate the principles of working together as women. Dropping into that healing place of peace and deep knowing—and sharing space in circle—the soul, or light, within each woman feels included, touched. Here she finds the rare opportunity to return to her inner self.

It is this work that I hope to convey here in this guide, so that perhaps you too may touch into the beauty and wonder of working in community, in circles, to support women, as they discover their resiliency, strength, and capacity to heal.[1]

As well, my intention is that this guide serve as a seed for remembering a deeper way to live, of

---

[1] I address women here in this guide not only because this is where my experience and commitment lies, but because there is a critical need at this time for women to live from the empowered place of their true nature. The earth—our world—cries out for the nourishment of the feminine, and this lives in women in a unique way. Yet clearly the principles in this guide can speak to all of us, men and women alike.

knowing one is always part of the fabric of the whole. Ultimately there is little difference between holding a group and staying present to one's life. Whatever the context, it is my wish that in reading this guide your own innate wisdom—your natural relatedness to all life—is revealed.

*The only appropriate response to life being in crisis
  on planet Earth*
*is to aim to be of service in its healing and
  regeneration.*
*In doing so we will begin to heal our disconnected
  and fractured selves*
*as we re-indigenize, reconnect, and reinhabit our
  place in the family of things*

— MARY OLIVER

THE CALL TO SERVE

If I could explain to you why I go each Wednesday to sit with a small circle of women who live in the safe-parking shelter in the small town where I live, I would say that I initially agreed to facilitate a group because I was curious to see if it would benefit the women to be together in an intimate circle where they are welcomed as they are. I had worked in women's shelters for years, but not in a safe-parking shelter, which is far less contained. Here, people living in their vehicles can find temporary residence in a fenced-in parking lot.

I would also say that I come, primarily, because of certain women who have deeply connected to what is offered. And I would invoke the words of Orland Bishop, who works with marginalized youth in Los Angeles, when he says, "when people are not welcomed, they go to the edges."

If you could sit next to me, this is what you would see. We sit in a circle around a vase of roses, geraniums, and lavender picked from my garden, set on the ground. A large white tent is above and around us. One day a storm brings intense winds, and the inside of the tent feels like a ship, with the tent walls as sails. The winds flap the walls wildly, as heavy rains drench the surrounding pavement. The following week, we bake in the heat. But still, we hold the circle, which includes the women who live in the village as well as some staff and volunteers.

⁓

Janet, who enters with her little dog, Sadie, sits on the worn, grey sofa next to a desk. During the opening check-in, she says quietly,

"I never knew it would be so difficult."

She is referring to the depth of her grief after the sudden loss of her daughter four months ago. She usually says little else during the groups. But one day she adds,

"I'm enjoying this circle." Like the sun peeking out from behind a cloud.

If you were present in this group, you would hear me speak in the beginning about listening, or perhaps stillness, or beauty. And then you would see the women sit in silence for five to ten minutes. You would see them close their eyes and follow a simple, guided meditation. Or, you might notice that some just sit quietly.

I am inwardly holding the women in my heart during this quiet time, even with the stream of cars passing on the road just outside the shelter. It's a natural gesture that I have done for many years, working with groups of women. And, I hold them as sacred.

I sing to the rivers and the hollows, to the places that have forgotten they are sacred. These are words I heard in a dream. I sometimes feel that our work in the circles is just this: a singing to the rivers and the hollows of the soul.

If we don't work at this depth, only the outer will change—and that change will perhaps not endure. When we work with what is inner, what is not visible, there healing and change takes place.

The earth is leaning sideways
and a song is emerging
from the floods and fires.
Urgent tendrils lift toward the sun.

You must be friends with silence to hear.
The songs of the guardians of silence
are the most powerful –
they are the most rare.

— JOY HARJO

FACILITATION

As facilitators we learn how to hold a space in a group of women, how to lead in a way that is non-hierarchical. We learn how to listen, and how to see with our heart. While some of us may have more stability in our outer circumstances, and even some training that enables us to hold space for others, we all face in some respect a longing for *home*. If not for a literal home, then for a place that feels like home, or for family, or inner nourishment.

Wherever we may be in our lives, holding the intention to come from the heart, practicing love and compassion towards ourselves in our own inner lives, and working on living from our center helps enrich the depth of our offering to others in circles.

We don't need to be fully "healed" to hold groups. Our own vulnerability, our own experience of suffering or woundedness can be an important unspoken note in the room that helps others.

What I have learned over the years of working with women is that I had to accept who I am—to be utterly myself—and that this simplicity allows others to change. "You need to value yourself," I was once told in a dream. "This is not a concept. It is *real*."

And what is real can speak wordlessly, for it is the foundation for any true change. How we relate to ourselves is powerfully linked to how we hold the other women. We are deeply connected, and so it follows that we need to include ourselves. And this applies not just to holding circles, but as well to how we live in relationship to others: to family and friends, strangers, and to the Earth herself.

Working With a Co-Facilitator

When I first began holding weekly circles for women in a day shelter, I held them on my own. I was curious to see how the circle could work. After a few months, I began to feel a certain strain of setting up the chairs, creating the centerpiece of flowers, holding the circle, listening, speaking. When I invited a colleague to join me, I discovered the value of having the presence of a co-facilitator, especially in challenging situations when my full attention was needed.

My initial colleague and I worked intuitively together. Due to her years of Zen meditation practice, she was familiar with silence. Sometimes, she would share her reflections and insights. A year later, other colleagues joined as co-facilitators at the shelter circles, each bringing their own unique contributions.

One of these was a woman who had little experience facilitating circles and rarely chose to speak, but she brought a particular quality of depth that was infinitely valuable. She knew how to hold an inner attention. Sometimes her eyes were closed, as in meditation, but other times, she would sit as you might imagine a rock, at the edge of a hillside. Her solidity and strength evoked a sense of relaxation and safety. It became evident to me that words were not always necessary in order to work together.

In many ways, the presence of two facilitators can work to create a felt sense of safety and containment. And while the circle is non-hierarchical, there is a need for one or both co-facilitators to help keep the focus.

*I've been considering the phrase, "all my relations,"
for some time now. It's hugely important. It's our
saving grace in the end. It points to the truth that we
are all related, that we are all connected, that we all
belong to each other. The most important word is
"all." Not just those who look like me, sing like me,
dance like me, speak like me, pray like me or behave
like me. ALL my relations. That means every person,
just as it means every rock, mineral, blade of grass,
and creature. We live because everything else does. If
we were to choose collectively to live that teaching,
the energy of our change of consciousness would heal
each of us—and heal the planet.*

— Dr. Paulette Steeves, (Cree-Metis)

WELCOMING

I see a woman enter, say something light to her, like, "It's so good to see you," or "I'm glad you could join us." She looks up, and in that moment I see if she is open, or grieving, or in inner pain. It's a way of reading her state of being, which comes as a simple knowing. I then welcome that part of her too. As the circle is still forming, and we are seated together, I am aware of each woman's expression, the way she sits, how she holds herself.

A recent dream I had speaks to this:

An Eritrean woman asks me if I want to know about women and healing. I say yes. She then says, "Read a woman's temperature when you first see her. Then read her temperature again as she moves towards you. And then hold her hand and feel the oneness."

After this dream, I became more aware of how I do read a woman's temperature, so to speak. And how as her attention begins to turn towards me, or to what I'm saying, it's possible to inwardly "hold her hand." I can feel it almost tangibly, this knowing of oneness. Like noticing the wind blowing through the leaves of the tree outside my window, bringing a sense of belonging. This focused attention can help a woman weave a way back to herself.

When all are seated, I take a moment of quiet during which I imagine each woman in my heart, individually, and also as a group.

While I do have a framework for the day, I know that this heartfelt welcoming is a form of nourishment that I can offer right up front, as if to a desired guest.

Some facilitators prefer more structure, which can be very helpful. (We have included a basic structure at the back of this guide.) But I have come to learn that within this space of welcoming, I can more easily notice if there is a need for me to bring up something ordinary but light, in order to bring ease to the women. Or whether I might need to take a pause, and then describe to the women what we will do in our hour together. For some may be in need of a sense of predictability and safety.

I then begin our check-in by asking why the women are here today, what they need or are looking for in our circle. Here's where I listen deeply to what the undercurrent is, to what I can speak about or do.

What I hear on a recent day is a longing for quiet, for calm, for a sense of peace. A truck rumbles by on the gravel. And then two men and a woman push a cart that clatters on the road by the corner where we sit. It doesn't interfere with the settling that's taking place among the women in our circle.

After the women have spoken, I say that we can focus now on a still place deep within our hearts, a place of sanctuary. As we go into meditation, the women close their eyes, and rest in this quality of space, with no effort. When it's time, I close with,

May peace be with us.

The soul speaks its truth only under quiet, inviting,
and trustworthy conditions.

— PARKER J. PALMER

Creating a Sense of Belonging

How do we create a sense of connectedness in a circle of women whom we have never met before? Or with whom we might have spoken only briefly, not knowing their history? Perhaps this story of my own experience can speak to your way of weaving together separate threads into a whole.

Years ago, I was invited to initiate a circle for women at The Living Room, a day shelter for women facing homelessness. I arrived for the first meeting on a cold, damp February morning. I imagined that I would be able to speak one-on-one with the women before we began, but that wasn't how it turned out.

⌒⌒

The program director leads me into a large, noise-filled room. She calls out for attention, and then somehow pushes me forward. I am now standing in front of about forty-five women.

All eyes are fixed on me, their faces without expression. I don't know what to say. So I hold up my book, *Women, Wisdom, & Dreams*. "I wrote this book," I begin, stalling for time. "It's about women and their dreams, and how we can find strength, healing, and nourishment from coming together in circles of listening and sharing, to help us meet the challenges we each face."

"And what I have learned in my years of listening to my own dreams and sitting with women in circles is that wherever the feminine touches—like a full moon shining down onto wounded parts of the earth herself, as I saw once in a dream—there is healing. And this healing is vitally important for all life because there is a deep sacredness within the feminine."

I realize, as I am speaking, that no one has ever before reflected to the women a sense of their own sacredness.

A stillness settles in the room. No one stirs. Their souls are listening, their personalities gone; they can taste a sense of something much larger. A sense of belonging has crept in, pushing aside any sense of shame or failure they've been carrying. "It was so quiet you could hear a pin drop," a staff member later confided to me. I see in their faces a deep relaxation for this brief moment.

⌒

Some of the women attending that day lived in shelters, others in their cars. Still others camped in the outdoors. They came to this day shelter where they were given hot meals, social services support, and help with securing housing and jobs. Sharing as I had seemed to have given them a larger context to their lives.

What happened in the room was not a method, a technique, or a special spiritual orientation. It involved accessing an empty, free space, and sharing from there. I know within myself this inner place of stillness, peace, and, wholeness, which is rarely found in everyday life. Resting here, I am able to resonate with, and meet, the women. And this seems to open a door to an inner space within them, a place of belonging.

To create sanctuary for a person is to take them outward of judgment of any kind, including the wanting to know their story. The [important] story, for me, is the future one. I want them to know there's a future in them first, before the past memory gets recalled. Because it's better to have a shared sense of purpose... and not just them telling me about their wounds, which does nothing for them or for me. The future sense needs awakening, in order to then contextualize the past.

— ORLAND BISHOP

⌒×

SANCTUARY

In the groups we offer a vision for new life, for a new way of being. Sometimes we catch glimpses of stories from the past, and then we listen. This way of listening requires that we put aside our thoughts of how to help or how to serve another. We simply listen with our heart, not just our ears. It's important not to dwell too heavily on the content of what is shared, as the group meeting is not therapy. Planting the seeds of new life is equally important.

We have come to trust that being listened to with compassion helps a woman to remember who she is, deeper than the wounds. Like a natural spring covered over by asphalt, images sometimes arise from within those depths. We hold these images without needing to understand them, so that the women can receive this inner healing support.

One woman arrived burdened by fear. In meditation, she saw the image of her brother who was no longer alive, reminding her how deeply he had loved and protected her when she was young. She hadn't thought about him for years. But now, she could feel and sense a place within her that made her feel safe to do so.

Another woman, during our writing practice, remembered the river she knew as a child. She wrote of the intimacy and joy of playing by this river, the sound of birds, cool water against her skin.

The sanctuary of the circle allows the inner self—the soul—to remember its true nature. These are just single moments, but over time, they build on one another, providing a foundation for a new source from which to live.

Once, a woman questioned me when she first came to a circle.

"This isn't a place where you tell us what to believe, is it? Because that's what they do at the other shelter. We have to read their books in order to stay there and get food."

"No," I laughed. "This circle is not such a place."

As a facilitator, our own suffering opens to a deeper, older knowledge about how to mend the threads of life that have been broken or torn apart. Our own vulnerability resonates like a clear note, speaking silently to others of our shared humanity.

When she first came, Marta, who had been shy to join initially, just listened and never spoke. Her eyes took in some deep form of nourishment that she was seeking. Then one day, she said,

"I come here because I learn here. I am learning." And then, weeks later, she told us, "I love this circle. I love you guys."

༈

I feel like I belong, for the first time.
This is a place where I belong.
I feel contented.

— SONJA, participant

To speak to the core...
to speak not always to what's shouting,
but to what's underneath
asking for nothing.

— AIDA LIMON

HOLDING SPACE

In this section we arrive at the very essence of Listening Circles—that "holding" a space is a dynamic way of being present, a way that opens to the possibility of transformation. Some call this space "grace." Others might describe it as a catalyst that makes things happen. Not in any outer way, but in the deeper terrain of our being, where subtle changes in the core of oneself first emerge.

How do we learn about holding, whether holding space, holding light, or holding family and each other? It can take time to uncover the power of our natural way of holding, especially because we have conditioning that teaches us that we have to make things happen. Yet the principle of holding space is adaptable to many situations. We hold a space in our heart and are willing to be in this place of not knowing, which is like holding open a door.

When the women are first arriving and chatting among themselves, I set a tone of inner, rather than outer, connection. I am aware of my breath, almost like a breathing prayer. This awareness of "the most holy" within oneself works like a tuning fork, calling everyone to the same note.

⤙

A young woman came to our circle for months before she spoke. One day, after the women wrote from a prompt, she offered to share what she had written. Reading quickly from her notebook, without looking up, she told a story about a girl. In her story she described how this girl had experienced great suffering that she had kept to herself all these years, without telling anyone. The other women in the circle sat completely still.

I remember looking at the women's faces, how intently they were listening, respectfully honoring the story as it flowed out from her notebook. The woman paused, taking a few deep breaths to steady her voice, and finished reading.

No one spoke. Everyone simply held the woman in the embrace of silence. Only then did another participant in the circle walk over to put her arm around her shoulders as she wept.

Wisdom, mercy, compassion. These are words I heard in a dream one night. And here these very qualities were rising naturally, a response to the wounds of another.

～

Imagine we have water, but no container. We need to find a glass or a cup to hold it, and only then can we drink from it. Every facilitator will find their own way of holding space. This is just one example to illustrate how it can work. At some point we begin to trust, to have the strength to bear the silence without filling it. And to see what is needed. No manual can show us how to do this, but hopefully the stories shared in this guide will evoke a memory of this natural, feminine way of working.

Silence opens us up to our inherent intelligence.

— ILARION MERCULIEFF,
Indigenous Aleut Elder, Alaskan Pribilof Islands

The Still Center

A few weeks after I facilitated a workshop for residents at the Bishop Ott Sweet Dreams Shelter for Women and Children in Baton Rouge, Louisiana, the program director commented, "It was a wonderful day. We've started to have fifteen minutes of silent meditation each morning. The women love the silence."

In our circles we always state that women can use whatever means they wish, or are comfortable with, to quiet their minds. Usually, we describe a simple heart meditation.

Even in these brief meditations of five to ten minutes, the women drop into a deep state within themselves—even those who have never experienced meditation.

This is a sacred time, when we sit in the nourishing silence and the women touch their own

33

quiet center. The facilitator is like a mediator between the inner and outer worlds. She holds the women silently in her heart. And while the sounds of traffic or cell phones or even construction may go on in the vicinity, it does not interfere with the feeling of peace.

And so we sit. When it's time to close, we conclude with a simple, "May peace be with us." Or simply, "Thank you."

We respect the quiet space immediately following meditation. Some women take a longer time to open their eyes. Others just sit quietly, looking at the flowers in the center of the room, or writing down a note so that they don't forget what they experienced. This too is a special time, when something from deep within can begin to take root.

In the quiet, in this brief meditation we offer, a quality of stillness infuses the circle. Often, it remains like a fragrance for the rest of our time together. I emphasize here the power, the beauty, of taking this time for women who are not accustomed to the silence.

One participant framed her experience of the circles as:

"...the sense of a sailboat 'righting' itself after leaning way over, or a ship coming back on course after having drifted off. That's the feeling I have so often in coming together in these circles. It helps me come back to my true course."

⌒✕

Carrying an Inner Note

As facilitators, we are always attentive to the seeds of renewal in the midst of devastation. For this creative capacity is in the earth, in each of us.

And yet, there are times when we have to navigate the fine line between holding what arises and stating a boundary. We need a boundary in order to define a space. The key is to create a focal point for the circle.

I usually begin with something like,

"Today, we will be exploring how we find strength."

Or I will tell a story in the beginning, to inwardly construct a boundary.

Even so, sometimes there is someone who will speak for a longer time, sharing more than others can digest. In such cases, I gently intervene and restore the focus. "Thank you," I might say. "We only have limited time, and we need to give an opportunity for others to share as well."

Imagine the circle as a source of nourishment, of returning to an inner home. And to protect, to keep this inner home safe, we need to include the aspect of the masculine that is in service to life. Traditional cultures understand this need for balance between the feminine and the masculine within. So we do need an awareness of holding a firm boundary that helps contain a sacred space for healing.

As facilitators, we learn to hold but not to impose. We learn to listen, to allow, and also we learn to protect the space and keep it clear. We hold a structure and protect the space.

Once, in our program at the day shelter, a woman was advised to come to our circle by the shelter's program director. She was afraid of sitting with other women in an intimate circle, and expressed her insecurity through an argumentative and disrespectful attitude. Clearly, she was disturbing the other women who had come seeking a safe space. Calmly, I told her that she could leave if she didn't want to be here.

She chose to stay. The atmosphere shifted, the disruption settled. After the meditation, her face was different, softer, perhaps even a bit bewildered.

"What *was* that?" she said. "Did I fall asleep?"

For the remainder of our time together, she sat quietly, mostly listening, sometimes sketching on the pad of paper on her lap.

Sometimes, a challenging situation becomes an opening.

Then in the deep silence,
wisdom begins to sing her unending
sunlit, inexpressible song,
the private song she sings to the solitary soul.

— THOMAS MERTON

MEDITATION

We always offer the meditation as an invitation. If someone does not want to meditate, or if they have a different way of being in the silence, we suggest they do whatever is familiar or comfortable. Each facilitator will express the purpose of meditation in his or her own way. I usually explain that meditation can calm the mind and help us to focus on the heart, which has a deeper wisdom.

Meditation of the Heart

Become aware of your breath, in and out, like gentle waves in the ocean. Now, think of someone you love. Or a time you were moved by nature, like watching a sunset or standing at the ocean. However you feel this love, which is unique to each of us, place this feeling in your heart. As thoughts arise in the mind, just drop them into your heart, one by one, like dropping pebbles into a pond.

And then we rest in the silence.

～✦

Our circles are not in the middle of a forest, but in cities and towns, filled with noise. So sometimes we hear the outside sounds of traffic, or children playing, or construction nearby. But the distraction of the sounds begins to fade, as the stillness grows deeper, more embracing.

At a certain point there is a change in the environment, like the calm that follows a sudden gust of wind. When we have "dropped in," a palpable sense of belonging and connection becomes present.

In the few minutes after I close the meditation, there is still a space of quiet that tenderly holds the women. Often, no one speaks, as if they want to remain a little longer in that peace. And then I might ask if anyone wants to share about their experience.

The peace that is now present has become woven into our time together, even as we move on to a time for sharing.

The last time at our circle I felt so peaceful. After the
silence, I talked about the pain in my heart. You
listened. This lifted something.
I feel no burden, no weight.
I feel so light, my heart is healing here.

— ALANA, newly homeless,
living in a shelter for one month

I come here for the quiet.
There's so much noise in the shelter,
and here I can be quiet, and listen inside.

— TERESE, participant

Sit and be still
until in the time of no rain
you hear beneath the dry wind's
commotion in the trees
the sound of flowing water among the rocks,
a stream unheard before,
and you are where breathing is prayer.

— Wendell Berry

WORK WITHOUT DOING

It is not what we do in these circles that really matters, but our state of being. In order to understand this knowledge, we need a framework, and for this, I offer here the following dream of mine.

I see three women standing in a park-like setting, by green leafing trees and a rocky hillside. They are singing a rich and wordless praise.

One of the women turns towards me and explains, "We don't do anything. We work vibrationally." She shows me a book they use for guidance. On the cover is written, "Women of the Sacred."

When I had this dream, it served as guidance for my own life, but also for my work with women of diverse backgrounds. The dream echoes the ancient Taoist understanding of *Wu Wei*, or "work without doing."

One warm spring day, at the edge of the safe-parking shelter, we sat under an awning near the corner of the property. I remember that day because it was a turning point. I came empty-handed, so to speak. I didn't know what we would talk about that day, and I didn't feel I had anything to offer. I had told the program director that we will focus on nourishment. But at this moment, I didn't know the way in.

I closed my eyes for a moment, while the women were settling into their chairs. The words of a prayer, like an intention of the heart, came to mind. *I do not ask to see, I do not ask to know, I ask only to be used.*

As I listen to the women speaking, I realize that real nourishment feeds the soul, and that this is what is sadly missing in our culture. I sit quietly for a moment, not imposing an idea or statement about nourishment. Instead, I am empty, waiting. And then, like catching a glimpse of a bird flying overhead, and following it in some way, I become aware of an experience I had when traveling as a photojournalist. I begin to tell this story, and the women seem to listen in a deep state of attention.

I tell them about my first real experience of nourishment many years ago, when I was traveling in

China. And about how I had not wanted to eat the meat that was served at every inn but instead had requested vegetarian food. On the last night of the trip, in a rural inn, I was the only person in the tour group who had not been served dinner. I waited for a long time. Finally, the cook walked into the dining room carrying a tray of a dozen vegetarian dishes.

The chef presented the food to me, then bowed deeply, and thanked me. He explained that he used to be the cook in a Buddhist monastery, and that it had been a long time since he was able to cook such dishes. And then he left. I could barely eat, I was so moved.

"You'd think," I said to the women, "that this would have made me happy. But instead, that night, I saw the image of the cook bowing to me, over and over again, and it broke my heart open." Somehow this image of the Buddhist chef's deep offering of respect cut through a lifetime's worth of protective defenses that had built up within me, and the deep nourishment of his gesture brought forth tears.

I stop speaking. The women are sitting silently, as if reflecting on what I have said. And then, they begin to share their own stories, one after the other, in the safety of the circle where nothing is judged. The quiet woman next to me says,

"It's like magic, how everyone feels so trusting. And this happens in just an hour. We feel at ease to share what we might not have ever spoken about before. I've never experienced this kind of depth."

This is work without doing. Not having an agenda, or interfering, but creating an intimate space where the circle can be nourished at a deep level. Not in literal food, although that's sometimes a wonderful offering at the end, but nourishment for the inner being—for the soul. In establishing a container where the women are free simply to be, where all is allowed and nothing is forced, we create a safe space in which seeds of renewal can be sown.

As a facilitator, we each find our way to knowing how to connect with the women. It's not the outer form, which does provide much needed structure, but the inner sustenance that comes through our willingness to be emptied, to listen for what appears, to surrender. And then we might notice that we can trust this older, inner knowledge.

Without my suffering, I wouldn't understand the suffering of others or be able to connect to them. My loneliness enables me to recognize the loneliness in other people, even when it's covered over; to find them where they have become lost in the dark, and sit with them; and to know that just by sitting with them, eventually they will find what they need in order to move forward.

— RACHEL NAOMI REMEN, M.D.

Witnessing

Recently, a psychologist from Bulgaria who had expressed interest in our women's circles wrote to me asking how I motivate the women participants. Her question activated in me a deeper question: *Why do these circles bring strength and a deep sense of value within, so that participants can live in the world in a different way?*

Pondering this led me to the concept of witnessing. As a facilitator, my work is simply to witness the lives of the women. Without judgment. Without a need to change. Without even a desire to motivate the women to "improve" themselves.

Witnessing, without fixing or commenting, is an act of love.

In these circles we see and honor the soul and spirit, or highest good, of each individual. This enables them to be in the world in a more grounded way. As we know that we ourselves can at times become off-centered or ungrounded, and thereby wind up participating in life in a distracted, perhaps anxious way, so can others. So just as we work to hold our own center, and find trust when facing life's hardships from that place inside us, we help the women learn to re-orient their focus by honoring and witnessing their center.

At the same time, we hold no expectations of results, whether for healing or resolution of life situations. Our work is not a promise for the healing of deep trauma.[2] It is simply to offer a focus on the sacred light within each woman. On that spark that exists in each, no matter their circumstances.

What we find is that when reflecting to the women their sacred nature—the place deep within that is inviolable, whole, a place that cannot be touched by outer experience—this place becomes a source of healing.

---

[2] Interestingly, however, professionals in the field of trauma recovery suggest that even 5-10 minutes of daily prayer or meditation can help address symptoms of Post Traumatic Stress Disorder (PTSD). And it has been found that calming the arousal systems in the deeper regions of the brain helps to calm PTSD more than verbal processing. (This calming is called "bottom-up processing" according to Bessel Van der Kolk, MD, trauma researcher and author.)

One day, Janet remembered a dream she had forty years ago. She had been a young woman at the time.

"I never told this dream to anyone," she says. After all these years, here was the right place for it to be received, and witnessed. While we rarely include dreams in the circles, this one came, unbidden, and I felt to welcome it.

Her dream spoke of a young woman who is lost and doesn't know where to find her path. And then, a great shining black horse appears. The girl has no fear as she mounts the horse and rides it through fields and prairies, with unrestrained joy.

I sat listening to her dream, to the wild beauty of this horse, its magnificence and power. I felt inside myself that somewhere this horse was Janet, and that sharing it was a powerful act of claiming this magnificence in front of the rest of us.

The other women in the circle remained quiet. We sat in this way, no one talking, holding this awareness of the horse being her own life essence, a quality that became covered over during hard times. Instinctually, we shared in the wordless recognition of the sacred in this moment.

Why did Janet remember this and share it in the container of the circle? Perhaps to reclaim in some way her own inner strength. I did not touch upon her dream again. I sensed that she just wanted to have it heard, not to have it analyzed or interpreted.

To witness another, to glimpse that inexpressible and sacred interior place, is healing in itself. It does not motivate a woman to change. But it does change her way of relating to life. It's like a linking up, a reuniting, of one's inner beauty with the outer world.

Because of this new connection, certain pathways open up that were previously blocked. And a natural consequence of this connection is to want to engage in life in a way that is more in line with one's deeper self.

Wendy Herschman, executive director of The Red Shoes, a nonprofit organization for women in Baton Rouge, Louisiana, commented after we held a workshop for women who were living in a nearby shelter for the unhoused:

"You honor their being, their soul and spirit. And it changes them so they can be in the world in a different way."

We witness through both our eyes and our heart. This touches the very core of a woman, the essence that perhaps was never witnessed, never acknowledged.

Once there was a flower.
A very lonely, lovely flower she was.
She looked around and seeing no other flowers
*   like herself,*
She began to feel very, very lonely.

One day a thistle came into bloom next door.
This was a very old and wise thistle that blossomed
*   through difficulty. But this made the medicine of*
*   the thistle even stronger.*

This medicine was so strong that it had awakened
*   something in the flower.*
Suddenly, the flower became more aware, slowly by
*   slowly, more and more aware.*

Then she noticed that she wasn't alone at all.
She saw ants in a line going by, little fliers in the air
*   and an occasional spider, caterpillar, worm or*
*   grasshopper.*

For the flower was never alone at all, in fact she was
*   somebody's habitat.*

— VICTORIA, a participant

WRITING

After the meditation, I often invite the women to do a free write, starting with a prompt I provide. I say,

"We have an opportunity to write now, if you'd like. In this exercise, we write freely, without judging or even thinking about it. Just let the words come—maybe there's a story, or a memory, or anything else that comes to you. Don't work at it, just let the words come."

Then I offer a prompt, such as *Once there was a seed*…to use as a starting point if they wish. The prompt usually connects the women to the earth, to nature, to life. For women who are uncomfortable with writing, I suggest they draw.

A few minutes into the exercise, the women can be taken into a deep and perhaps unfamiliar inner landscape. Often we hear afterwards, "I didn't know I could write!"

Seven or eight minutes later, I invite the women to wrap up the writing, which is now flowing freely. When all have finished, I invite anyone who would like to share what they wrote. The womens' words, and their stories, are welcomed in this safe space.

Mostly, we receive their sharing in silence, although I thank each woman after she has read aloud. Her inner thoughts and feelings are deeply welcomed and respected.

Through this whole process we catch threads of an inner, guiding force that offers direction, awareness, and strength. Even for those who don't choose to write, or share. For simply being part of the circle as witness offers an experience of inner belonging.

Sometimes, I notice that a woman sits with pen in hand, paused as if waiting. Or she might write a few sentences but then stop. This happened recently, when an older woman who never wanted to sit with us in a circle found the courage to join. She clearly didn't want to write. But during the time when others read what they had written, she felt safe enough to tell a story about her life as a child, here in this small town where we live. She described her mother and the different houses they lived in.

Now in her sixties, she lives in her car. The case manager earlier mentioned to me that this woman struggles with addiction. We listen with all of our attention. This type of deep listening offers a bridge from there to here. From what is carried from the past to now. The listening is dynamic. Often, it is enough simply that a woman feels valued and heard.

Sometimes, such as in this case, the sharing goes even deeper, as if a woman speaks from an inner place that is bare, like a tree in winter. When this happens, we are all equally touched. The listening field itself is enlarged and blessed by such a share, one that requires courage, and inspires compassion. These small moments seem as if to touch gold on the inner planes—they may not even turn into anything overt, but they are a true witnessing of Life. Life so longs to be seen, heard, honored.

⌒

Another time, a participant wrote about the wind, reading aloud for the first time. There was a sense of wonder as we listened:

Once there was a wind. It was a southwest wind and it was blowing pretty good.

The leaves on the trees were flapping around and were making a beautiful song.

The grass on the land was making a beautiful swishing sound in the waters as the waves that blew up on the land were making a beautiful music.

And when they all listened they were making an absolutely beautiful sound together.

— MABEL, participant

This exercise connects a woman to her deeper knowing, to a sense of vastness or connectedness inside, which she usually doesn't have access to, or whose existence she is unaware of. This place of inner creativity gives hope and possibility to the women.

"I love the writing," Mabel commented. Usually withdrawn, often having a hard time finding words, she, like some others, expresses herself most easily in this way, through the writing, and the reading of it. For some, this self-expression involves touching an ancestral memory. For others, there is a connection to a deep source of stability and beauty. Practiced over time, these writing sessions become healing exercises, woven with words and feeling.

⌒

One day, I suggest beginning the writing with, *Once there was an ocean*. As we live thirty minutes from the Pacific Ocean, I trust that most of the women have experienced the coast here. I don't expect anything but wait to see if the women are able to relate to this prompt. I wait in silence as the women write.

After five minutes, I invite them to read if they wish. No one speaks up. So we wait some more, and finally, Lena says, "I'll read, I guess. It isn't much." Lena reads in a measured, slow pace:

A woman stands by the ocean. I see the waves, and behind them is a place of calm, of peace. That is who I am, and I feel that the chaos of the crashing waves is when I am with people.

She nods, as if affirming this realization about her own nature. It seems to calm her, and she smiles.

Finding this creative place within her has opened a new window into herself.

In our circles, we use prompts that connect us to nature, to the earth:

Once there was a sunflower...

Once there was a tree...

Once there was a wind...

Once there was a river...

Once there was an ocean...

Once there was a seed...

These are powerful entry points into our inner lives. When the women have developed a sense of comfort and safety in the circle, we might suggest starting with, *Once there was a girl.*

Regardless of the prompt, I am always aware of an unseen, abiding grace that leads the women to a story of healing through these practices.

Offering Poems or Prose Excerpts

Sometimes it's a good idea to bring in some new energy, as this helps moisten the ground for the women's own creative expression. It is subtle work to access what lies hidden, to touch those places that are normally quite buried. And it takes time to release the seeds that provide an opportunity for something to be revealed.

So on occasion, I bring in an inspiring poem or prose excerpt to read. One woman has said she liked the freedom of being able to write what she wanted with this exercise. Until I introduced this practice, she had not written with the prompts. Instead, she would make a sketch while the others were quietly writing. For some, using poetry as a starting point opens a door to a depth of feeling, a sense of spaciousness without restriction.

The first time I brought a poem to the circle at the safe-parking shelter, I wasn't sure if the women would be receptive. I mentioned that the poet, Nikita Gill, a young British-Indian writer, was rejected by 137 publishers. She then turned to social media to share her poetry, and now has over half a million followers.

The poet's conviction touches the women, opening them to the power of poetry. I began to read:

Your Soft Heart[3]

You are still the child who gently places
Fallen baby birds back in their nests.
You are still the soft soul that gets
Your heart broken over cruel words
And awful acts when you watch the news.
You are still the gentle heart who once
Tried to heal a flower by attempting to stick
Its petals back on when ignorant feet
    trampled it.

This is why you are important.
This is why you will always be needed.

Kindness is the greatest endangered thing.
And here you are, existing, with your heart so
    full with it.

After reading, I suggest that the participants can write from a word or phrase that touched them. Sometimes, some of the women take the initiative to

---

[3] From *Where Hope Comes From: Poems of Resilience, Healing, and Light* (2021)

write their own form of poetry. I sit quietly, while the women write. Some facilitators like to write during this time. I use this time to breathe with awareness, holding the women inwardly.

Beauty Contemplation

At other times, I bring in photographs of flowers or nature, and lay them on the ground in the center of the circle. *Choose an image that speaks to you*, I say to the women.

Mei confides to me one day, after coming to the circle for several months, that she is Chinese, from Vietnam. After the war, she moved to the United States to live with her husband, but the relationship ended. She became homeless one year ago.

Mei comes regularly to our weekly circles. She is quiet and rarely speaks up during the meetings. Today, I have laid in the center of the circle some close-up photographs of flowers. I decided to offer these images before meditation, which is different than how I usually structure our time together. I do this because the atmosphere is heavy today, dense, and I feel that the images of beauty might bring a quality of upliftment. I ask them to each choose one they like.

Mei selects an image of a yellow wildflower and holds it on her lap during the five minutes of silent meditation or contemplation. After the silence, the women write about the particular flower they have selected. After the writing time is up, I ask, *Does anyone want to share what they've written?* Mei, usually so reserved, jumps in:

"Some people have tried to make me feel bad about myself. They try to put me down. I realized, when we were meditating, that this flower is me. "

Reflecting on Nature

One week, at the safe-parking shelter, I sense that the image of a tree will help the women to feel more connected to their own sense of self. To their innate qualities that belong solely to them.

We sit outside in the corner of the lot under the canopy of several old oak trees. I have placed a green cloth circling round a vase of leaves and rosemary from my yard. Today several village residents and three volunteers join us.

After meditation, we have forty-five minutes remaining. I sit for a moment, feeling the warmth of the sun on my back in the early fall. I ask the women if they want to write or speak. One of the women, a veteran, says that she can't write much because of an injury to her hand. So I suggest that instead of writing, we choose a tree, each of us, that might represent us. Or, at the least, that might have qualities that we need, or feel an affinity towards.

I begin the sharing. I talk about a birch tree I see every day. The birch has delicate branches that move easily in the wind, and there are often two crows that sit on the top. Every day my daughter and granddaughter and I look for the crows, and they are always in the same position, often preening or just observing. They see us. We see them.

The women go around the circle. One chooses a redwood. Another the oak, the sequoia, the willow. When they describe the qualities of their tree, they bring awareness to their relationship to these deeper qualities they long for, or that are already in them, waiting to be valued.

The women are enjoying this revelation. One woman, who usually speaks with long pauses between thoughts, begins to describe the oak.

"I love the oak. I've seen the oak have branches that come out and nearly touch the ground. Then the branch rises up towards the sun. It just needed to rest. Then it could grow upwards again. It just needed a rest."

Another woman speaks of the weeping willow, about its empathy, how it protects those beneath its branches. She says,

"I connect with people this way too. Both with homeless people and not homeless people. The people I sometimes try to comfort may think, 'Like, I'm worthy of someone noticing me?' My caring is kind of like a protection."

As the women share, they listen to one another, and they listen to themselves. They become accustomed to, even trusting of, the knowing that comes from a place deeper than their circumstances, deeper than their wounds.

Just as we are about to leave, a volunteer asks Stella if she finished the writing she began a week ago. Stella nods. The volunteer asks if she'd read it. Stella takes out her journal, and unlike in the past, when she dismissed or apologized for her writing, she is now willing, ready. I had given a prompt last week about open space, such as a field, or an ocean.

Once there was an open space... Stella opens her notebook, searches for the writing. Her little black-and-white dog shifts on her lap as she begins to read in a steady, measured way.

Once upon a time there were the plains, the greenness. It was vast, and on this land was so much life. There were great herds of buffalo, of wild horses, and smaller groupings of deer and elk. There was land as far as the eye could see.

There were no farms, no houses, and no towns. There were some big circles of rocks, called teepee rings left on the ground as the only proof that people had been here previously. The Native Americans put them around the house of their lodges to stop the cold breeze of air from blowing through. They would use them again if they returned in the future. They were oftentimes located around lakes or rivers. Especially if they planned on staying for some time.

The plains were beautiful. The sunrises and sunsets were awesome to see. And there was nothing to stand in your way. Just the openness of it all. All you could see in every direction. How beautiful.

Stella is impartial, almost impersonal as she reads. When I listen, I hear her describe a living vastness as if she has known this herself. Is this an ancestral memory? It's not for me to ask. The other women are also deeply moved. The traffic, the clucking of a few chickens in a field on the other side of the fence, the rumbling of a truck along the street, all this fades. I feel all thoughts are stilled. There is just this quality of peace for the moment, as we listen.

When she finishes, there is silence. She shrugs and says only that she enjoys the writing.

〜

I see, again and again, how simple this practice of writing is, how the quiet nourishment it brings seeps into the crevices and cracks, moistening those places within that are waiting, like seeds.

Once there was a seed named Carmen.
I was a seed that needed to germinate and
in order to do that,
I needed to experience life. Well, here I am.

I had been through trials and tribulations.
Over time I am finally coming into my
own.

I am like hundreds of women, as I finally
found a deeper power to help me
achieve the impossibles of life.

And this has been a light.
I let It into my life and soul.
And I love It.

— CARMEN, participant

Silence is not the absence of something,
but the presence of everything.

— GORDON HEMPTON

Structuring a Circle

Setup

Chairs should be arranged in a circle, with a simple center that is made beautiful in some way. This can involve spreading a cloth or textile on the ground, and in its center, placing a special 'speaking object' for the women to hold when they speak, such as a stone or shell. We often bring a small vase of flowers or moss from the branches of a tree and, when appropriate, a candle.

We also come prepared with paper and pens to distribute. At the safe-parking shelter, a staff member bought journals for each woman to keep.

Speaking Stone

During times of sharing, we offer the women a polished stone, or a shell, which they hold in their hands when they wish to say something. Holding the stone creates a sense of safety for the woman, for while holding it she has the floor, so to speak.

When she is holding the stone in her hands, feeling its smooth surface, looking at it quietly, no one else speaks. This gives a breathing space, a time to listen within, without any sense of unease with the silent moments before words come. Sometimes, a woman might hold the stone for a minute and realize that she has nothing she wants to say at that moment. We often speak of the power of listening—this too is valued.

Circle Guidelines

We recommend these guidelines in order to create a safe container for the circles. Sometimes it's necessary to state the guidelines before we begin, especially if it is the first time we are meeting together. Most of the time there is no need, as the women are used to gathering in respect for one another.

This is a shared container where we get to touch the space and silence that lives within us all, and be nourished by it.

- What is shared in this circle remains confidential.

- We speak and listen from the heart.

- We ask for no cross-talk when someone is using the speaking stone.

- We listen to each other with curiosity, compassion, and courtesy.

- We respect each other's contributions by keeping comments fairly brief, so others can share.

- We encourage everyone to speak or share, but each is free to be quiet when they wish.

- We ask that sharing be from our own experience in life.

- At times we may ask you to come back to your own lived experience if the conversation strays to more outward topics.

Circle Components

After welcoming the women, I explain briefly the simple structure of the meeting, especially if there are new participants. This creates a feeling of safety, of knowing both what will happen and that there will be no imposition on the women. Timing is up to the facilitator, but here are some examples of what has worked.

Facilitator Introduction

This can be very simple. It might include why we offer these circles, and our experience. One co-facilitator I worked with for many years always said the same thing, and it wove into the meetings like a thread of trust: "Many years ago my Buddhist teacher told me that my work is to help women find their true strength. I love these circles. It's always an honor to sit with women in this way."

Check-in (5 minutes)

We invite the participants to say their names and to share, if they wish, what brings them here today, or what their intention or hope is for the meeting. This usually lasts no more than five minutes.

Meditation (5–10 minutes)

While an earlier chapter offers specific suggestions for leading meditation, you may also wish to find your own way of inviting the silence.

Group Sharing (5–10 minutes)

After meditation, the atmosphere is quite still and deep. After a few minutes of resting in this quiet, I hold up the talking stone and ask if anyone would like to speak about their experience in meditation. Perhaps an image or feeling came up during the time of silence that they would like to share. Sometimes, there is no desire among the women to speak. We then move on to a creative practice, which also holds the silence, in a different way.

Writing or other creative practice (15–20 minutes)

We discussed in the previous chapter the practices of writing, reading of short excerpts, and nature or beauty contemplation. Feel free to follow your intuition and experiment with what works best for those in the circle.

Working With Time

Our circles last for one hour, and we finish promptly.

When the participants feel the inner structure of the circle being held by the facilitator, they feel safe to be themselves. Occasionally, a woman will speak without awareness of the need to respect the timeframe of the circle. While rare, if it does occur, a facilitator needs to find her own way of creating a boundary with respect to time. We might need to step in by kindly thanking the participant for her sharing, and say that we need to move on to make room for others who might wish to share.

The facilitator needs to listen within herself to determine what is most needed in these situations. On occasion, there might be a sense to wait until a woman finishes sharing, even if it's a long and winding path before she comes to a conclusion. At such times, it is as if a woman is excavating her inner life, trying to locate the gold. And so we wait. We listen.

Closing

When the hour is nearly over, I say that our time together is nearly at a close. I thank the women for meeting, and sometimes, in summary, I touch upon the themes that came up that day.

I might then suggest taking a few deep breaths, and then sit for a minute of silence. This brief moment of silence is itself a container. It's a space that can hold what had been talked about and shared, and what was felt deeply during the hour. Usually there is quality of stillness while one also becomes aware of the sounds outside. It is an important step before the return to the needs of the day.

At other times, we ask the women if there is a word, or words, that come to mind to describe their experience of the circle today. This is another way to bring a sense of closing to the intimacy and depth of our time together. The women can speak freely here, without the use of a talking stone or object.

You might hear something like this as words flow readily around the circle:

I feel peace.

My mind feels clear.

I'm just grateful to be here.

Gratitude.

Calm.

I'm just happy to be with you all. I look forward to it every week.

⌒➤

Some facilitators like to incorporate a practice of gratitude at the end of our time together. Each woman offers something that she is grateful for, bringing the circle to a close.

At first, however, I was reluctant to ask the women. I was aware of keeping the circle free of imposition of any kind. But what happened was this. One day I said,

"We have just a few minutes left. If you wish, we can each say one thing that we're grateful for."

No one spoke for a few moments. Then Pat, who recently found housing, said she was grateful for the group of women sitting here. That coming each week helped her to get through her last year. The others began to speak as well. For a brother. Or a grandmother in Mexico. Mostly for the circle of women. And I saw how deeply gratitude lives, and that it needs a breathing space, an invitation, and is itself a form of nourishment.

At such times, a space opens up in which our listening naturally deepens, broadens, to include not just each woman but the soft breeze that has just arrived, or the sound of traffic in the distance. In its own way, this simple gesture of gratitude weaves us back into life.

I had a vision that the ancestors told us to heal the world.

When we heal ourselves, we also heal our ancestors, our grandmothers, our grandfathers, and our children.

When we heal ourselves, we also heal Mother Earth.

— Dr. Rita Pitka Blumenstein, Yup'ik Elder

The Field of Nourishment

Listening Circles have made a huge difference for those women who are receptive and somewhere longing to experience more deeply who they are. In a way, it is a longing for their own light, or soul. It might be covered over and hidden—but the sacred nature of a woman always lies waiting to be recognized. It cannot be otherwise. It is like the sacredness of a river or a mountain, or a child who reaches up and puts their hand in yours. A connection with something essential and real. Many women who are depressed or lonely have this longing and have no way to understand that it is life calling us to live more deeply, from the heart.

Very rarely is this kind of remembering work done alone. We are like branches of a tree, interconnected, and therefore our healing and our strength comes from relationships, both within oneself and with others. And we reflect back and forth to each other, so if you see my light, it is a reflection of your own light.

Do not be concerned by the number of women that come to a circle. My experience is that no matter who was the facilitator of those we trained, there was usually a consistent number of women, ranging from six to ten, but sometimes smaller. Sometimes the smaller circles of women created such an intimacy and sense of safety that the depth of sharing was astonishing. And in that heartfelt space, grace was present. Like a sweetness that filled the hollows of one's despair.

What is important is to feel the joy of coming together, no matter the difficulties present. Whether a woman comes just once or returns again and again, everyone benefits. There are always some women for whom these circles offer a lifeline. Rarely did they know what they hungered for. Maybe it was a depression or, as one woman described, a dark hole that she couldn't climb out of. For others, the circle affirms their longing to be valued, to connect with others at this deep core level, and to heal a collective denial of the sacredness of women.

On a hot afternoon during a heat wave at the safe-parking shelter, with just a tarp overhead to give us shade, a volunteer brings food to share at the end of our meeting. We have ended our meeting with a moment of silence and a deep peace settles in this circle of seven women. The volunteer then reaches into her bag and offers a frozen popsicle to each of us. This gesture of nourishment reflects the field of nourishment we establish.

As a tree needs sun and water in order to live, so too we need a certain kind of inner nourishment. This we have forgotten in the urgency for solutions to the crises we face. Here in these simple circles we offer sustenance that can help to heal and bring change in a community.

I hope that this small guide will support you in your own endeavors, helping serve the urgent need that is everywhere to honor the sacredness of women and all of life.

ACKNOWLEDGMENTS

I am deeply grateful to Barbara Lee, who made it possible for us to hold a women's Listening Circle at Horizon Shine Village. I am also grateful for the dedication of volunteers Molly Munro and Barbara Renzullo, who contributed to the on-going stability of our group meetings by participating in the circle week after week.

A deep acknowledgement of Celeste Austin, Director of Special Programs at The Living Room Day Shelter for Women in Santa Rosa, where I had the opportunity to spearhead and ground this important work with women on the margins. Without her sponsorship this work would not have evolved to where it is today, or served the many women it has.

I offer my gratitude to Orland Bishop, founder of ShadeTree Multicultural Foundation for the light of wisdom and inspiration he offers from his work with youth suffering at the margins in Los Angeles. And I am deeply grateful to Kahontakwas Diane Longboat, Turtle Clan, Mohawk Nation, a ceremonial leader, traditional teacher and healer, and professional educator who has served as an Elder for the Centre for Addiction and Mental Health since 2013, for her encouragement. My gratitude as well to Ilarion Merculieff at the Global Center for Indigenous Leadership and Lifeways for his deep understanding of the need at this time for the healing medicine of silence that the feminine brings. With appreciation to Claire Noble, for her insights and suggestions in the final stage of writing.

Also, to those who gave so generously in offering the financial support needed to bring this guide into completion—my heartfelt appreciation.

Last but certainly not least, to the many women who have opened their hearts and minds, and offered their trust and their deep wisdom in participating in these Listening Circles: I thank you from my heart.

About The Author

ANNE SCOTT, founder of DreamWeather Foundation, has led workshops and retreats for women in diverse communities and organizations around the country and internationally. The focus of her work is on restoring the link between feminine wisdom and social change, and the healing nature of dreams. Anne was a speaker at the United Nations Peace Initiative in Geneva, Switzerland, and a global conference in Jaipur, India, "Making Way for the Feminine for the Benefit of the World Community."

Anne is the author of several books, including *Finding Home: Restoring the Sacred to Life* and *Women, Wisdom & Dreams: The Light of the Feminine Soul.* She began working with groups of newly homeless women in shelters in 2010. The core of her work is restoring the sacred to life through embodying feminine wisdom.

You can reach Anne at:

DreamWeather Foundation
PO Box 2002
Sebastopol, CA 95473
info@dreamweather.org
www.dreamweather.org

DIANA BADGER has been a writer, editor, and content developer for four decades. She served as lead facilitator and program manager for DreamWeather's Listening With the Heart program at The Living Room Day Shelter for Women in Santa Rosa, CA, from 2014-2020. She has also facilitated therapeutic groups at San Quentin Prison, where she served as curriculum manager and designer for the Insight Garden Program. Since 2020 she has held her own women's circle focused on Spiritual Ecology, and practices as a counseling archetypal astrologer.